Precious Metals Trader's Portfolio

JAMES F. HATCHER III

ISBN-13: 978-1981765720
ISBN-10: 1981765727

Available from Amazon.com, CreateSpace.com,
and other retail outlets.

Published by The Masonic Press.
Find more interesting titles on our website:

masonicpress.com

Printed by CreateSpace, Charleston, SC
An Amazon.com Company

METAL/TYPE:_____ Exchange:_____

DATE	BUY @ PRICE	BUY AMOUNT	WEIGHT	SELL @ PRICE	SELL AMOUNT	PROFIT/LOSS

METAL/TYPE:_____ Exchange:_____

DATE	BUY @ PRICE	BUY AMOUNT	WEIGHT	SELL @ PRICE	SELL AMOUNT	PROFIT/LOSS

METAL/TYPE:_____ Exchange:_____

DATE	BUY @ PRICE	BUY AMOUNT	WEIGHT	SELL @ PRICE	SELL AMOUNT	PROFIT/LOSS

METAL/TYPE:_____ Exchange:_____

DATE	BUY @ PRICE	BUY AMOUNT	WEIGHT	SELL @ PRICE	SELL AMOUNT	PROFIT/LOSS

METAL/TYPE:_____ Exchange:_____

DATE	BUY @ PRICE	BUY AMOUNT	WEIGHT	SELL @ PRICE	SELL AMOUNT	PROFIT/LOSS

METAL/TYPE:_____ Exchange:_____

DATE	BUY @ PRICE	BUY AMOUNT	WEIGHT	SELL @ PRICE	SELL AMOUNT	PROFIT/LOSS

METAL/TYPE:_____ Exchange:_____

DATE	BUY @ PRICE	BUY AMOUNT	WEIGHT	SELL @ PRICE	SELL AMOUNT	PROFIT/LOSS

METAL/TYPE:_____ Exchange:_____

DATE	BUY @ PRICE	BUY AMOUNT	WEIGHT	SELL @ PRICE	SELL AMOUNT	PROFIT/LOSS

METAL/TYPE:_____ Exchange:_____

DATE	BUY @ PRICE	BUY AMOUNT	WEIGHT	SELL @ PRICE	SELL AMOUNT	PROFIT/LOSS

METAL/TYPE:_____ Exchange:_____

DATE	BUY @ PRICE	BUY AMOUNT	WEIGHT	SELL @ PRICE	SELL AMOUNT	PROFIT/LOSS

METAL/TYPE:_____ Exchange:_____

DATE	BUY @ PRICE	BUY AMOUNT	WEIGHT	SELL @ PRICE	SELL AMOUNT	PROFIT/LOSS

METAL/TYPE:_____ Exchange:_____

DATE	BUY @ PRICE	BUY AMOUNT	WEIGHT	SELL @ PRICE	SELL AMOUNT	PROFIT/LOSS

METAL/TYPE:_____ Exchange:_____

DATE	BUY @ PRICE	BUY AMOUNT	WEIGHT	SELL @ PRICE	SELL AMOUNT	PROFIT/LOSS

METAL/TYPE:_____ Exchange:_____

DATE	BUY @ PRICE	BUY AMOUNT	WEIGHT	SELL @ PRICE	SELL AMOUNT	PROFIT/LOSS

METAL/TYPE:_____ Exchange:_____

DATE	BUY @ PRICE	BUY AMOUNT	WEIGHT	SELL @ PRICE	SELL AMOUNT	PROFIT/LOSS

METAL/TYPE:_____ Exchange:_____

DATE	BUY @ PRICE	BUY AMOUNT	WEIGHT	SELL @ PRICE	SELL AMOUNT	PROFIT/LOSS

METAL/TYPE:_____ Exchange:_____

DATE	BUY @ PRICE	BUY AMOUNT	WEIGHT	SELL @ PRICE	SELL AMOUNT	PROFIT/LOSS

METAL/TYPE:_____ Exchange:_____

DATE	BUY @ PRICE	BUY AMOUNT	WEIGHT	SELL @ PRICE	SELL AMOUNT	PROFIT/LOSS

METAL/TYPE:_____ Exchange:_____

DATE	BUY @ PRICE	BUY AMOUNT	WEIGHT	SELL @ PRICE	SELL AMOUNT	PROFIT/LOSS

METAL/TYPE:_____ Exchange:_____

DATE	BUY @ PRICE	BUY AMOUNT	WEIGHT	SELL @ PRICE	SELL AMOUNT	PROFIT/LOSS

METAL/TYPE:_____ Exchange:_____

DATE	BUY @ PRICE	BUY AMOUNT	WEIGHT	SELL @ PRICE	SELL AMOUNT	PROFIT/LOSS

METAL/TYPE:_____ Exchange:_____

DATE	BUY @ PRICE	BUY AMOUNT	WEIGHT	SELL @ PRICE	SELL AMOUNT	PROFIT/LOSS

METAL/TYPE:_____ Exchange:_____

DATE	BUY @ PRICE	BUY AMOUNT	WEIGHT	SELL @ PRICE	SELL AMOUNT	PROFIT/LOSS

METAL/TYPE:_____ Exchange:_____

DATE	BUY @ PRICE	BUY AMOUNT	WEIGHT	SELL @ PRICE	SELL AMOUNT	PROFIT/LOSS

METAL/TYPE:_____ Exchange:_____

DATE	BUY @ PRICE	BUY AMOUNT	WEIGHT	SELL @ PRICE	SELL AMOUNT	PROFIT/LOSS

METAL/TYPE:_____ Exchange:_____

DATE	BUY @ PRICE	BUY AMOUNT	WEIGHT	SELL @ PRICE	SELL AMOUNT	PROFIT/LOSS

METAL/TYPE:_____ Exchange:_____

DATE	BUY @ PRICE	BUY AMOUNT	WEIGHT	SELL @ PRICE	SELL AMOUNT	PROFIT/LOSS

METAL/TYPE:_____ Exchange:_____

DATE	BUY @ PRICE	BUY AMOUNT	WEIGHT	SELL @ PRICE	SELL AMOUNT	PROFIT/LOSS

METAL/TYPE:_____ Exchange:_____

DATE	BUY @ PRICE	BUY AMOUNT	WEIGHT	SELL @ PRICE	SELL AMOUNT	PROFIT/LOSS

METAL/TYPE:_____ Exchange:_____

DATE	BUY @ PRICE	BUY AMOUNT	WEIGHT	SELL @ PRICE	SELL AMOUNT	PROFIT/LOSS

METAL/TYPE:_____ Exchange:_____

DATE	BUY @ PRICE	BUY AMOUNT	WEIGHT	SELL @ PRICE	SELL AMOUNT	PROFIT/LOSS

METAL/TYPE:_____ Exchange:_____

DATE	BUY @ PRICE	BUY AMOUNT	WEIGHT	SELL @ PRICE	SELL AMOUNT	PROFIT/LOSS

METAL/TYPE:_____ Exchange:_____

DATE	BUY @ PRICE	BUY AMOUNT	WEIGHT	SELL @ PRICE	SELL AMOUNT	PROFIT/LOSS

METAL/TYPE:_____ Exchange:_____

DATE	BUY @ PRICE	BUY AMOUNT	WEIGHT	SELL @ PRICE	SELL AMOUNT	PROFIT/LOSS

METAL/TYPE:_____ Exchange:_____

DATE	BUY @ PRICE	BUY AMOUNT	WEIGHT	SELL @ PRICE	SELL AMOUNT	PROFIT/LOSS

METAL/TYPE:_____ Exchange:_____

DATE	BUY @ PRICE	BUY AMOUNT	WEIGHT	SELL @ PRICE	SELL AMOUNT	PROFIT/LOSS

METAL/TYPE:_____ Exchange:_____

DATE	BUY @ PRICE	BUY AMOUNT	WEIGHT	SELL @ PRICE	SELL AMOUNT	PROFIT/LOSS

METAL/TYPE:_____ Exchange:_____

DATE	BUY @ PRICE	BUY AMOUNT	WEIGHT	SELL @ PRICE	SELL AMOUNT	PROFIT/LOSS

METAL/TYPE:_____ Exchange:_____

DATE	BUY @ PRICE	BUY AMOUNT	WEIGHT	SELL @ PRICE	SELL AMOUNT	PROFIT/LOSS

METAL/TYPE:_____ Exchange:_____

DATE	BUY @ PRICE	BUY AMOUNT	WEIGHT	SELL @ PRICE	SELL AMOUNT	PROFIT/LOSS

METAL/TYPE:_____ Exchange:_____

DATE	BUY @ PRICE	BUY AMOUNT	WEIGHT	SELL @ PRICE	SELL AMOUNT	PROFIT/LOSS

METAL/TYPE:_____ Exchange:_____

DATE	BUY @ PRICE	BUY AMOUNT	WEIGHT	SELL @ PRICE	SELL AMOUNT	PROFIT/LOSS

METAL/TYPE:_____ Exchange:_____

DATE	BUY @ PRICE	BUY AMOUNT	WEIGHT	SELL @ PRICE	SELL AMOUNT	PROFIT/LOSS

METAL/TYPE:_____ Exchange:_____

DATE	BUY @ PRICE	BUY AMOUNT	WEIGHT	SELL @ PRICE	SELL AMOUNT	PROFIT/LOSS

METAL/TYPE:_____ Exchange:_____

DATE	BUY @ PRICE	BUY AMOUNT	WEIGHT	SELL @ PRICE	SELL AMOUNT	PROFIT/LOSS

METAL/TYPE:_____ Exchange:_____

DATE	BUY @ PRICE	BUY AMOUNT	WEIGHT	SELL @ PRICE	SELL AMOUNT	PROFIT/LOSS

METAL/TYPE:_____ Exchange:_____

DATE	BUY @ PRICE	BUY AMOUNT	WEIGHT	SELL @ PRICE	SELL AMOUNT	PROFIT/LOSS

METAL/TYPE:_____ Exchange:_____

DATE	BUY @ PRICE	BUY AMOUNT	WEIGHT	SELL @ PRICE	SELL AMOUNT	PROFIT/LOSS

METAL/TYPE:_____ Exchange:_____

DATE	BUY @ PRICE	BUY AMOUNT	WEIGHT	SELL @ PRICE	SELL AMOUNT	PROFIT/LOSS

METAL/TYPE:_____ Exchange:_____

DATE	BUY @ PRICE	BUY AMOUNT	WEIGHT	SELL @ PRICE	SELL AMOUNT	PROFIT/LOSS

METAL/TYPE:_____ Exchange:_____

DATE	BUY @ PRICE	BUY AMOUNT	WEIGHT	SELL @ PRICE	SELL AMOUNT	PROFIT/LOSS

METAL/TYPE:_____ Exchange:_____

DATE	BUY @ PRICE	BUY AMOUNT	WEIGHT	SELL @ PRICE	SELL AMOUNT	PROFIT/LOSS

METAL/TYPE:_____ Exchange:_____

DATE	BUY @ PRICE	BUY AMOUNT	WEIGHT	SELL @ PRICE	SELL AMOUNT	PROFIT/LOSS

METAL/TYPE:_____ Exchange:_____

DATE	BUY @ PRICE	BUY AMOUNT	WEIGHT	SELL @ PRICE	SELL AMOUNT	PROFIT/LOSS

METAL/TYPE:_____ Exchange:_____

DATE	BUY @ PRICE	BUY AMOUNT	WEIGHT	SELL @ PRICE	SELL AMOUNT	PROFIT/LOSS

METAL/TYPE:_____ Exchange:_____

DATE	BUY @ PRICE	BUY AMOUNT	WEIGHT	SELL @ PRICE	SELL AMOUNT	PROFIT/LOSS

METAL/TYPE:_____ Exchange:_____

DATE	BUY @ PRICE	BUY AMOUNT	WEIGHT	SELL @ PRICE	SELL AMOUNT	PROFIT/LOSS

METAL/TYPE:_____ Exchange:_____

DATE	BUY @ PRICE	BUY AMOUNT	WEIGHT	SELL @ PRICE	SELL AMOUNT	PROFIT/LOSS

METAL/TYPE:_____ Exchange:_____

DATE	BUY @ PRICE	BUY AMOUNT	WEIGHT	SELL @ PRICE	SELL AMOUNT	PROFIT/LOSS

METAL/TYPE:_____ Exchange:_____

DATE	BUY @ PRICE	BUY AMOUNT	WEIGHT	SELL @ PRICE	SELL AMOUNT	PROFIT/LOSS

METAL/TYPE:_____ Exchange:_____

DATE	BUY @ PRICE	BUY AMOUNT	WEIGHT	SELL @ PRICE	SELL AMOUNT	PROFIT/LOSS

METAL/TYPE:_____ Exchange:_____

DATE	BUY @ PRICE	BUY AMOUNT	WEIGHT	SELL @ PRICE	SELL AMOUNT	PROFIT/LOSS

METAL/TYPE:_____ Exchange:_____

DATE	BUY @ PRICE	BUY AMOUNT	WEIGHT	SELL @ PRICE	SELL AMOUNT	PROFIT/LOSS

METAL/TYPE:_____ Exchange:_____

DATE	BUY @ PRICE	BUY AMOUNT	WEIGHT	SELL @ PRICE	SELL AMOUNT	PROFIT/LOSS

METAL/TYPE:_____ Exchange:_____

DATE	BUY @ PRICE	BUY AMOUNT	WEIGHT	SELL @ PRICE	SELL AMOUNT	PROFIT/LOSS

METAL/TYPE:_____ Exchange:_____

DATE	BUY @ PRICE	BUY AMOUNT	WEIGHT	SELL @ PRICE	SELL AMOUNT	PROFIT/LOSS

METAL/TYPE:_____ Exchange:_____

DATE	BUY @ PRICE	BUY AMOUNT	WEIGHT	SELL @ PRICE	SELL AMOUNT	PROFIT/LOSS

METAL/TYPE:_____ Exchange:_____

DATE	BUY @ PRICE	BUY AMOUNT	WEIGHT	SELL @ PRICE	SELL AMOUNT	PROFIT/LOSS

METAL/TYPE:_____ Exchange:_____

DATE	BUY @ PRICE	BUY AMOUNT	WEIGHT	SELL @ PRICE	SELL AMOUNT	PROFIT/LOSS

METAL/TYPE:_____ Exchange:_____

DATE	BUY @ PRICE	BUY AMOUNT	WEIGHT	SELL @ PRICE	SELL AMOUNT	PROFIT/LOSS

METAL/TYPE:_____ Exchange:_____

DATE	BUY @ PRICE	BUY AMOUNT	WEIGHT	SELL @ PRICE	SELL AMOUNT	PROFIT/LOSS

METAL/TYPE:_____ Exchange:_____

DATE	BUY @ PRICE	BUY AMOUNT	WEIGHT	SELL @ PRICE	SELL AMOUNT	PROFIT/LOSS

METAL/TYPE:_____ Exchange:_____

DATE	BUY @ PRICE	BUY AMOUNT	WEIGHT	SELL @ PRICE	SELL AMOUNT	PROFIT/LOSS

METAL/TYPE:_____ Exchange:_____

DATE	BUY @ PRICE	BUY AMOUNT	WEIGHT	SELL @ PRICE	SELL AMOUNT	PROFIT/LOSS

METAL/TYPE:_____ Exchange:_____

DATE	BUY @ PRICE	BUY AMOUNT	WEIGHT	SELL @ PRICE	SELL AMOUNT	PROFIT/LOSS

METAL/TYPE:_____ Exchange:_____

DATE	BUY @ PRICE	BUY AMOUNT	WEIGHT	SELL @ PRICE	SELL AMOUNT	PROFIT/LOSS

METAL/TYPE:_____ Exchange:_____

DATE	BUY @ PRICE	BUY AMOUNT	WEIGHT	SELL @ PRICE	SELL AMOUNT	PROFIT/LOSS

METAL/TYPE:_____ Exchange:_____

DATE	BUY @ PRICE	BUY AMOUNT	WEIGHT	SELL @ PRICE	SELL AMOUNT	PROFIT/LOSS

METAL/TYPE:_____ Exchange:_____

DATE	BUY @ PRICE	BUY AMOUNT	WEIGHT	SELL @ PRICE	SELL AMOUNT	PROFIT/LOSS

METAL/TYPE:_____ Exchange:_____

DATE	BUY @ PRICE	BUY AMOUNT	WEIGHT	SELL @ PRICE	SELL AMOUNT	PROFIT/LOSS

METAL/TYPE:_____ Exchange:_____

DATE	BUY @ PRICE	BUY AMOUNT	WEIGHT	SELL @ PRICE	SELL AMOUNT	PROFIT/LOSS

METAL/TYPE:_____ Exchange:_____

DATE	BUY @ PRICE	BUY AMOUNT	WEIGHT	SELL @ PRICE	SELL AMOUNT	PROFIT/LOSS

METAL/TYPE:_____ Exchange:_____

DATE	BUY @ PRICE	BUY AMOUNT	WEIGHT	SELL @ PRICE	SELL AMOUNT	PROFIT/LOSS

METAL/TYPE:_____ Exchange:_____

DATE	BUY @ PRICE	BUY AMOUNT	WEIGHT	SELL @ PRICE	SELL AMOUNT	PROFIT/LOSS

METAL/TYPE:_____ Exchange:_____

DATE	BUY @ PRICE	BUY AMOUNT	WEIGHT	SELL @ PRICE	SELL AMOUNT	PROFIT/LOSS

METAL/TYPE:_____ Exchange:_____

DATE	BUY @ PRICE	BUY AMOUNT	WEIGHT	SELL @ PRICE	SELL AMOUNT	PROFIT/LOSS

METAL/TYPE:_____ Exchange:_____

DATE	BUY @ PRICE	BUY AMOUNT	WEIGHT	SELL @ PRICE	SELL AMOUNT	PROFIT/LOSS

METAL/TYPE:_____ Exchange:_____

DATE	BUY @ PRICE	BUY AMOUNT	WEIGHT	SELL @ PRICE	SELL AMOUNT	PROFIT/LOSS

METAL/TYPE:_____ Exchange:_____

DATE	BUY @ PRICE	BUY AMOUNT	WEIGHT	SELL @ PRICE	SELL AMOUNT	PROFIT/LOSS

METAL/TYPE:_____ Exchange:_____

DATE	BUY @ PRICE	BUY AMOUNT	WEIGHT	SELL @ PRICE	SELL AMOUNT	PROFIT/LOSS

METAL/TYPE:_____ Exchange:_____

DATE	BUY @ PRICE	BUY AMOUNT	WEIGHT	SELL @ PRICE	SELL AMOUNT	PROFIT/LOSS

METAL/TYPE:_____ Exchange:_____

DATE	BUY @ PRICE	BUY AMOUNT	WEIGHT	SELL @ PRICE	SELL AMOUNT	PROFIT/LOSS

METAL/TYPE:_____ Exchange:_____

DATE	BUY @ PRICE	BUY AMOUNT	WEIGHT	SELL @ PRICE	SELL AMOUNT	PROFIT/LOSS

METAL/TYPE:_____ Exchange:_____

DATE	BUY @ PRICE	BUY AMOUNT	WEIGHT	SELL @ PRICE	SELL AMOUNT	PROFIT/LOSS

METAL/TYPE:_____ Exchange:_____

DATE	BUY @ PRICE	BUY AMOUNT	WEIGHT	SELL @ PRICE	SELL AMOUNT	PROFIT/LOSS

METAL/TYPE:_____ Exchange:_____

DATE	BUY @ PRICE	BUY AMOUNT	WEIGHT	SELL @ PRICE	SELL AMOUNT	PROFIT/LOSS

METAL/TYPE:_____ Exchange:_____

DATE	BUY @ PRICE	BUY AMOUNT	WEIGHT	SELL @ PRICE	SELL AMOUNT	PROFIT/LOSS

METAL/TYPE:_____ Exchange:_____

DATE	BUY @ PRICE	BUY AMOUNT	WEIGHT	SELL @ PRICE	SELL AMOUNT	PROFIT/LOSS

METAL/TYPE:_____ Exchange:_____

DATE	BUY @ PRICE	BUY AMOUNT	WEIGHT	SELL @ PRICE	SELL AMOUNT	PROFIT/LOSS

METAL/TYPE:_____ Exchange:_____

DATE	BUY @ PRICE	BUY AMOUNT	WEIGHT	SELL @ PRICE	SELL AMOUNT	PROFIT/LOSS

METAL/TYPE:_____ Exchange:_____

DATE	BUY @ PRICE	BUY AMOUNT	WEIGHT	SELL @ PRICE	SELL AMOUNT	PROFIT/LOSS

METAL/TYPE:_____ Exchange:_____

DATE	BUY @ PRICE	BUY AMOUNT	WEIGHT	SELL @ PRICE	SELL AMOUNT	PROFIT/LOSS

METAL/TYPE:_____ Exchange:_____

DATE	BUY @ PRICE	BUY AMOUNT	WEIGHT	SELL @ PRICE	SELL AMOUNT	PROFIT/LOSS

METAL/TYPE:_____ Exchange:_____

DATE	BUY @ PRICE	BUY AMOUNT	WEIGHT	SELL @ PRICE	SELL AMOUNT	PROFIT/LOSS

METAL/TYPE:_____ Exchange:_____

DATE	BUY @ PRICE	BUY AMOUNT	WEIGHT	SELL @ PRICE	SELL AMOUNT	PROFIT/LOSS

METAL/TYPE:_____ Exchange:_____

DATE	BUY @ PRICE	BUY AMOUNT	WEIGHT	SELL @ PRICE	SELL AMOUNT	PROFIT/LOSS

METAL/TYPE:_____ Exchange:_____

DATE	BUY @ PRICE	BUY AMOUNT	WEIGHT	SELL @ PRICE	SELL AMOUNT	PROFIT/LOSS

METAL/TYPE:_____ Exchange:_____

DATE	BUY @ PRICE	BUY AMOUNT	WEIGHT	SELL @ PRICE	SELL AMOUNT	PROFIT/LOSS

METAL/TYPE:_____ Exchange:_____

DATE	BUY @ PRICE	BUY AMOUNT	WEIGHT	SELL @ PRICE	SELL AMOUNT	PROFIT/LOSS

METAL/TYPE:_____ Exchange:_____

DATE	BUY @ PRICE	BUY AMOUNT	WEIGHT	SELL @ PRICE	SELL AMOUNT	PROFIT/LOSS

METAL/TYPE:_____ Exchange:_____

DATE	BUY @ PRICE	BUY AMOUNT	WEIGHT	SELL @ PRICE	SELL AMOUNT	PROFIT/LOSS

METAL/TYPE:_____ Exchange:_____

DATE	BUY @ PRICE	BUY AMOUNT	WEIGHT	SELL @ PRICE	SELL AMOUNT	PROFIT/LOSS

METAL/TYPE:_____ Exchange:_____

DATE	BUY @ PRICE	BUY AMOUNT	WEIGHT	SELL @ PRICE	SELL AMOUNT	PROFIT/LOSS

METAL/TYPE:_____ Exchange:_____

DATE	BUY @ PRICE	BUY AMOUNT	WEIGHT	SELL @ PRICE	SELL AMOUNT	PROFIT/LOSS

METAL/TYPE:_____ Exchange:_____

DATE	BUY @ PRICE	BUY AMOUNT	WEIGHT	SELL @ PRICE	SELL AMOUNT	PROFIT/LOSS

METAL/TYPE:_____ Exchange:_____

DATE	BUY @ PRICE	BUY AMOUNT	WEIGHT	SELL @ PRICE	SELL AMOUNT	PROFIT/LOSS

METAL/TYPE:_____ Exchange:_____

DATE	BUY @ PRICE	BUY AMOUNT	WEIGHT	SELL @ PRICE	SELL AMOUNT	PROFIT/LOSS

METAL/TYPE:_____ Exchange:_____

DATE	BUY @ PRICE	BUY AMOUNT	WEIGHT	SELL @ PRICE	SELL AMOUNT	PROFIT/LOSS

METAL/TYPE:_____ Exchange:_____

DATE	BUY @ PRICE	BUY AMOUNT	WEIGHT	SELL @ PRICE	SELL AMOUNT	PROFIT/LOSS

METAL/TYPE:_____ Exchange:_____

DATE	BUY @ PRICE	BUY AMOUNT	WEIGHT	SELL @ PRICE	SELL AMOUNT	PROFIT/LOSS

METAL/TYPE:_____ Exchange:_____

DATE	BUY @ PRICE	BUY AMOUNT	WEIGHT	SELL @ PRICE	SELL AMOUNT	PROFIT/LOSS

METAL/TYPE:_____ Exchange:_____

DATE	BUY @ PRICE	BUY AMOUNT	WEIGHT	SELL @ PRICE	SELL AMOUNT	PROFIT/LOSS

METAL/TYPE:_____ Exchange:_____

DATE	BUY @ PRICE	BUY AMOUNT	WEIGHT	SELL @ PRICE	SELL AMOUNT	PROFIT/LOSS

METAL/TYPE:_____ Exchange:_____

DATE	BUY @ PRICE	BUY AMOUNT	WEIGHT	SELL @ PRICE	SELL AMOUNT	PROFIT/LOSS

METAL/TYPE:_____ Exchange:_____

DATE	BUY @ PRICE	BUY AMOUNT	WEIGHT	SELL @ PRICE	SELL AMOUNT	PROFIT/LOSS

METAL/TYPE:_____ Exchange:_____

DATE	BUY @ PRICE	BUY AMOUNT	WEIGHT	SELL @ PRICE	SELL AMOUNT	PROFIT/LOSS

METAL/TYPE:_____ Exchange:_____

DATE	BUY @ PRICE	BUY AMOUNT	WEIGHT	SELL @ PRICE	SELL AMOUNT	PROFIT/LOSS

METAL/TYPE:_____ Exchange:_____

DATE	BUY @ PRICE	BUY AMOUNT	WEIGHT	SELL @ PRICE	SELL AMOUNT	PROFIT/LOSS

METAL/TYPE:_____ Exchange:_____

DATE	BUY @ PRICE	BUY AMOUNT	WEIGHT	SELL @ PRICE	SELL AMOUNT	PROFIT/LOSS

METAL/TYPE:_____ Exchange:_____

DATE	BUY @ PRICE	BUY AMOUNT	WEIGHT	SELL @ PRICE	SELL AMOUNT	PROFIT/LOSS

METAL/TYPE:_____ Exchange:_____

DATE	BUY @ PRICE	BUY AMOUNT	WEIGHT	SELL @ PRICE	SELL AMOUNT	PROFIT/LOSS

METAL/TYPE:_____ Exchange:_____

DATE	BUY @ PRICE	BUY AMOUNT	WEIGHT	SELL @ PRICE	SELL AMOUNT	PROFIT/LOSS

METAL/TYPE:_____ Exchange:_____

DATE	BUY @ PRICE	BUY AMOUNT	WEIGHT	SELL @ PRICE	SELL AMOUNT	PROFIT/LOSS

METAL/TYPE:_____ Exchange:_____

DATE	BUY @ PRICE	BUY AMOUNT	WEIGHT	SELL @ PRICE	SELL AMOUNT	PROFIT/LOSS

METAL/TYPE:_____ Exchange:_____

DATE	BUY @ PRICE	BUY AMOUNT	WEIGHT	SELL @ PRICE	SELL AMOUNT	PROFIT/LOSS

METAL/TYPE:_____ Exchange:_____

DATE	BUY @ PRICE	BUY AMOUNT	WEIGHT	SELL @ PRICE	SELL AMOUNT	PROFIT/LOSS

METAL/TYPE:_____ Exchange:_____

DATE	BUY @ PRICE	BUY AMOUNT	WEIGHT	SELL @ PRICE	SELL AMOUNT	PROFIT/LOSS

METAL/TYPE:_____ Exchange:_____

DATE	BUY @ PRICE	BUY AMOUNT	WEIGHT	SELL @ PRICE	SELL AMOUNT	PROFIT/LOSS

METAL/TYPE:_____ Exchange:_____

DATE	BUY @ PRICE	BUY AMOUNT	WEIGHT	SELL @ PRICE	SELL AMOUNT	PROFIT/LOSS

METAL/TYPE:_____ Exchange:_____

DATE	BUY @ PRICE	BUY AMOUNT	WEIGHT	SELL @ PRICE	SELL AMOUNT	PROFIT/LOSS

METAL/TYPE:_____ Exchange:_____

DATE	BUY @ PRICE	BUY AMOUNT	WEIGHT	SELL @ PRICE	SELL AMOUNT	PROFIT/LOSS

METAL/TYPE:_____ Exchange:_____

DATE	BUY @ PRICE	BUY AMOUNT	WEIGHT	SELL @ PRICE	SELL AMOUNT	PROFIT/LOSS

METAL/TYPE:_____ Exchange:_____

DATE	BUY @ PRICE	BUY AMOUNT	WEIGHT	SELL @ PRICE	SELL AMOUNT	PROFIT/LOSS

METAL/TYPE:_____ Exchange:_____

DATE	BUY @ PRICE	BUY AMOUNT	WEIGHT	SELL @ PRICE	SELL AMOUNT	PROFIT/LOSS

METAL/TYPE:_____ Exchange:_____

DATE	BUY @ PRICE	BUY AMOUNT	WEIGHT	SELL @ PRICE	SELL AMOUNT	PROFIT/LOSS

METAL/TYPE:_____ Exchange:_____

DATE	BUY @ PRICE	BUY AMOUNT	WEIGHT	SELL @ PRICE	SELL AMOUNT	PROFIT/LOSS

METAL/TYPE:_____ Exchange:_____

DATE	BUY @ PRICE	BUY AMOUNT	WEIGHT	SELL @ PRICE	SELL AMOUNT	PROFIT/LOSS

METAL/TYPE:_____ Exchange:_____

DATE	BUY @ PRICE	BUY AMOUNT	WEIGHT	SELL @ PRICE	SELL AMOUNT	PROFIT/LOSS

METAL/TYPE:_____ Exchange:_____

DATE	BUY @ PRICE	BUY AMOUNT	WEIGHT	SELL @ PRICE	SELL AMOUNT	PROFIT/LOSS

METAL/TYPE:_____ Exchange:_____

DATE	BUY @ PRICE	BUY AMOUNT	WEIGHT	SELL @ PRICE	SELL AMOUNT	PROFIT/LOSS

METAL/TYPE:_____ Exchange:_____

DATE	BUY @ PRICE	BUY AMOUNT	WEIGHT	SELL @ PRICE	SELL AMOUNT	PROFIT/LOSS

METAL/TYPE:_____ Exchange:_____

DATE	BUY @ PRICE	BUY AMOUNT	WEIGHT	SELL @ PRICE	SELL AMOUNT	PROFIT/LOSS

METAL/TYPE:_____ Exchange:_____

DATE	BUY @ PRICE	BUY AMOUNT	WEIGHT	SELL @ PRICE	SELL AMOUNT	PROFIT/LOSS

METAL/TYPE:_____ Exchange:_____

DATE	BUY @ PRICE	BUY AMOUNT	WEIGHT	SELL @ PRICE	SELL AMOUNT	PROFIT/LOSS

METAL/TYPE:_____ Exchange:_____

DATE	BUY @ PRICE	BUY AMOUNT	WEIGHT	SELL @ PRICE	SELL AMOUNT	PROFIT/LOSS

METAL/TYPE:_____ Exchange:_____

DATE	BUY @ PRICE	BUY AMOUNT	WEIGHT	SELL @ PRICE	SELL AMOUNT	PROFIT/LOSS

METAL/TYPE:_____ Exchange:_____

DATE	BUY @ PRICE	BUY AMOUNT	WEIGHT	SELL @ PRICE	SELL AMOUNT	PROFIT/LOSS

METAL/TYPE:_____ Exchange:_____

DATE	BUY @ PRICE	BUY AMOUNT	WEIGHT	SELL @ PRICE	SELL AMOUNT	PROFIT/LOSS

METAL/TYPE:_____ Exchange:_____

DATE	BUY @ PRICE	BUY AMOUNT	WEIGHT	SELL @ PRICE	SELL AMOUNT	PROFIT/LOSS

METAL/TYPE:_____ Exchange:_____

DATE	BUY @ PRICE	BUY AMOUNT	WEIGHT	SELL @ PRICE	SELL AMOUNT	PROFIT/LOSS

METAL/TYPE:_____ Exchange:_____

DATE	BUY @ PRICE	BUY AMOUNT	WEIGHT	SELL @ PRICE	SELL AMOUNT	PROFIT/LOSS

METAL/TYPE:_____ Exchange:_____

DATE	BUY @ PRICE	BUY AMOUNT	WEIGHT	SELL @ PRICE	SELL AMOUNT	PROFIT/LOSS

METAL/TYPE:_____ Exchange:_____

DATE	BUY @ PRICE	BUY AMOUNT	WEIGHT	SELL @ PRICE	SELL AMOUNT	PROFIT/LOSS

METAL/TYPE:_____ Exchange:_____

DATE	BUY @ PRICE	BUY AMOUNT	WEIGHT	SELL @ PRICE	SELL AMOUNT	PROFIT/LOSS

METAL/TYPE:_____ Exchange:_____

DATE	BUY @ PRICE	BUY AMOUNT	WEIGHT	SELL @ PRICE	SELL AMOUNT	PROFIT/LOSS

METAL/TYPE:_____ Exchange:_____

DATE	BUY @ PRICE	BUY AMOUNT	WEIGHT	SELL @ PRICE	SELL AMOUNT	PROFIT/LOSS

METAL/TYPE:_____ Exchange:_____

DATE	BUY @ PRICE	BUY AMOUNT	WEIGHT	SELL @ PRICE	SELL AMOUNT	PROFIT/LOSS

METAL/TYPE:_____ Exchange:_____

DATE	BUY @ PRICE	BUY AMOUNT	WEIGHT	SELL @ PRICE	SELL AMOUNT	PROFIT/LOSS

METAL/TYPE:_____ Exchange:_____

DATE	BUY @ PRICE	BUY AMOUNT	WEIGHT	SELL @ PRICE	SELL AMOUNT	PROFIT/LOSS

METAL/TYPE:_____ Exchange:_____

DATE	BUY @ PRICE	BUY AMOUNT	WEIGHT	SELL @ PRICE	SELL AMOUNT	PROFIT/LOSS

METAL/TYPE:_____ Exchange:_____

DATE	BUY @ PRICE	BUY AMOUNT	WEIGHT	SELL @ PRICE	SELL AMOUNT	PROFIT/LOSS

METAL/TYPE:_____ Exchange:_____

DATE	BUY @ PRICE	BUY AMOUNT	WEIGHT	SELL @ PRICE	SELL AMOUNT	PROFIT/LOSS

METAL/TYPE:_____ Exchange:_____

DATE	BUY @ PRICE	BUY AMOUNT	WEIGHT	SELL @ PRICE	SELL AMOUNT	PROFIT/LOSS

METAL/TYPE:_____ Exchange:_____

DATE	BUY @ PRICE	BUY AMOUNT	WEIGHT	SELL @ PRICE	SELL AMOUNT	PROFIT/LOSS

METAL/TYPE:_____ Exchange:_____

DATE	BUY @ PRICE	BUY AMOUNT	WEIGHT	SELL @ PRICE	SELL AMOUNT	PROFIT/LOSS

METAL/TYPE:_____ Exchange:_____

DATE	BUY @ PRICE	BUY AMOUNT	WEIGHT	SELL @ PRICE	SELL AMOUNT	PROFIT/LOSS

METAL/TYPE:_____ Exchange:_____

DATE	BUY @ PRICE	BUY AMOUNT	WEIGHT	SELL @ PRICE	SELL AMOUNT	PROFIT/LOSS

METAL/TYPE:_____ Exchange:_____

DATE	BUY @ PRICE	BUY AMOUNT	WEIGHT	SELL @ PRICE	SELL AMOUNT	PROFIT/LOSS

METAL/TYPE:_____ Exchange:_____

DATE	BUY @ PRICE	BUY AMOUNT	WEIGHT	SELL @ PRICE	SELL AMOUNT	PROFIT/LOSS

METAL/TYPE:_____ Exchange:_____

DATE	BUY @ PRICE	BUY AMOUNT	WEIGHT	SELL @ PRICE	SELL AMOUNT	PROFIT/LOSS

METAL/TYPE:_____ Exchange:_____

DATE	BUY @ PRICE	BUY AMOUNT	WEIGHT	SELL @ PRICE	SELL AMOUNT	PROFIT/LOSS

METAL/TYPE:_____ Exchange:_____

DATE	BUY @ PRICE	BUY AMOUNT	WEIGHT	SELL @ PRICE	SELL AMOUNT	PROFIT/LOSS

METAL/TYPE:_____ Exchange:_____

DATE	BUY @ PRICE	BUY AMOUNT	WEIGHT	SELL @ PRICE	SELL AMOUNT	PROFIT/LOSS

METAL/TYPE:_____ Exchange:_____

DATE	BUY @ PRICE	BUY AMOUNT	WEIGHT	SELL @ PRICE	SELL AMOUNT	PROFIT/LOSS

METAL/TYPE:_____ Exchange:_____

DATE	BUY @ PRICE	BUY AMOUNT	WEIGHT	SELL @ PRICE	SELL AMOUNT	PROFIT/LOSS

METAL/TYPE:_____ Exchange:_____

DATE	BUY @ PRICE	BUY AMOUNT	WEIGHT	SELL @ PRICE	SELL AMOUNT	PROFIT/LOSS

METAL/TYPE:_____ Exchange:_____

DATE	BUY @ PRICE	BUY AMOUNT	WEIGHT	SELL @ PRICE	SELL AMOUNT	PROFIT/LOSS

METAL/TYPE:_____ Exchange:_____

DATE	BUY @ PRICE	BUY AMOUNT	WEIGHT	SELL @ PRICE	SELL AMOUNT	PROFIT/LOSS

METAL/TYPE:_____ Exchange:_____

DATE	BUY @ PRICE	BUY AMOUNT	WEIGHT	SELL @ PRICE	SELL AMOUNT	PROFIT/LOSS

METAL/TYPE:_____ Exchange:_____

DATE	BUY @ PRICE	BUY AMOUNT	WEIGHT	SELL @ PRICE	SELL AMOUNT	PROFIT/LOSS

METAL/TYPE:_____ Exchange:_____

DATE	BUY @ PRICE	BUY AMOUNT	WEIGHT	SELL @ PRICE	SELL AMOUNT	PROFIT/LOSS

METAL/TYPE:_____ Exchange:_____

DATE	BUY @ PRICE	BUY AMOUNT	WEIGHT	SELL @ PRICE	SELL AMOUNT	PROFIT/LOSS

METAL/TYPE:_____ Exchange:_____

DATE	BUY @ PRICE	BUY AMOUNT	WEIGHT	SELL @ PRICE	SELL AMOUNT	PROFIT/LOSS

METAL/TYPE:_____ Exchange:_____

DATE	BUY @ PRICE	BUY AMOUNT	WEIGHT	SELL @ PRICE	SELL AMOUNT	PROFIT/LOSS

METAL/TYPE:_____ Exchange:_____

DATE	BUY @ PRICE	BUY AMOUNT	WEIGHT	SELL @ PRICE	SELL AMOUNT	PROFIT/LOSS

METAL/TYPE:_____ Exchange:_____

DATE	BUY @ PRICE	BUY AMOUNT	WEIGHT	SELL @ PRICE	SELL AMOUNT	PROFIT/LOSS

METAL/TYPE:_____ Exchange:_____

DATE	BUY @ PRICE	BUY AMOUNT	WEIGHT	SELL @ PRICE	SELL AMOUNT	PROFIT/LOSS

METAL/TYPE:_____ Exchange:_____

DATE	BUY @ PRICE	BUY AMOUNT	WEIGHT	SELL @ PRICE	SELL AMOUNT	PROFIT/LOSS

METAL/TYPE:_____ Exchange:_____

DATE	BUY @ PRICE	BUY AMOUNT	WEIGHT	SELL @ PRICE	SELL AMOUNT	PROFIT/LOSS

METAL/TYPE:_____ Exchange:_____

DATE	BUY @ PRICE	BUY AMOUNT	WEIGHT	SELL @ PRICE	SELL AMOUNT	PROFIT/LOSS

METAL/TYPE:_____ Exchange:_____

DATE	BUY @ PRICE	BUY AMOUNT	WEIGHT	SELL @ PRICE	SELL AMOUNT	PROFIT/LOSS

METAL/TYPE:_____ Exchange:_____

DATE	BUY @ PRICE	BUY AMOUNT	WEIGHT	SELL @ PRICE	SELL AMOUNT	PROFIT/LOSS

METAL/TYPE:_____ Exchange:_____

DATE	BUY @ PRICE	BUY AMOUNT	WEIGHT	SELL @ PRICE	SELL AMOUNT	PROFIT/LOSS

METAL/TYPE:_____ Exchange:_____

DATE	BUY @ PRICE	BUY AMOUNT	WEIGHT	SELL @ PRICE	SELL AMOUNT	PROFIT/LOSS

METAL/TYPE:_____ Exchange:_____

DATE	BUY @ PRICE	BUY AMOUNT	WEIGHT	SELL @ PRICE	SELL AMOUNT	PROFIT/LOSS

METAL/TYPE:_____ Exchange:_____

DATE	BUY @ PRICE	BUY AMOUNT	WEIGHT	SELL @ PRICE	SELL AMOUNT	PROFIT/LOSS

METAL/TYPE:_____ Exchange:_____

DATE	BUY @ PRICE	BUY AMOUNT	WEIGHT	SELL @ PRICE	SELL AMOUNT	PROFIT/LOSS

METAL/TYPE:_____ Exchange:_____

DATE	BUY @ PRICE	BUY AMOUNT	WEIGHT	SELL @ PRICE	SELL AMOUNT	PROFIT/LOSS

METAL/TYPE:_____ Exchange:_____

DATE	BUY @ PRICE	BUY AMOUNT	WEIGHT	SELL @ PRICE	SELL AMOUNT	PROFIT/LOSS

METAL/TYPE:_____ Exchange:_____

DATE	BUY @ PRICE	BUY AMOUNT	WEIGHT	SELL @ PRICE	SELL AMOUNT	PROFIT/LOSS

METAL/TYPE:_____ Exchange:_____

DATE	BUY @ PRICE	BUY AMOUNT	WEIGHT	SELL @ PRICE	SELL AMOUNT	PROFIT/LOSS

METAL/TYPE:_____ Exchange:_____

DATE	BUY @ PRICE	BUY AMOUNT	WEIGHT	SELL @ PRICE	SELL AMOUNT	PROFIT/LOSS

METAL/TYPE:_____ Exchange:_____

DATE	BUY @ PRICE	BUY AMOUNT	WEIGHT	SELL @ PRICE	SELL AMOUNT	PROFIT/LOSS

METAL/TYPE:_____ Exchange:_____

DATE	BUY @ PRICE	BUY AMOUNT	WEIGHT	SELL @ PRICE	SELL AMOUNT	PROFIT/LOSS

METAL/TYPE:_____ Exchange:_____

DATE	BUY @ PRICE	BUY AMOUNT	WEIGHT	SELL @ PRICE	SELL AMOUNT	PROFIT/LOSS

METAL/TYPE:_____ Exchange:_____

DATE	BUY @ PRICE	BUY AMOUNT	WEIGHT	SELL @ PRICE	SELL AMOUNT	PROFIT/LOSS

METAL/TYPE:_____ Exchange:_____

DATE	BUY @ PRICE	BUY AMOUNT	WEIGHT	SELL @ PRICE	SELL AMOUNT	PROFIT/LOSS

METAL/TYPE:_____ Exchange:_____

DATE	BUY @ PRICE	BUY AMOUNT	WEIGHT	SELL @ PRICE	SELL AMOUNT	PROFIT/LOSS

METAL/TYPE:_____ Exchange:_____

DATE	BUY @ PRICE	BUY AMOUNT	WEIGHT	SELL @ PRICE	SELL AMOUNT	PROFIT/LOSS

METAL/TYPE:_____ Exchange:_____

DATE	BUY @ PRICE	BUY AMOUNT	WEIGHT	SELL @ PRICE	SELL AMOUNT	PROFIT/LOSS

METAL/TYPE:_____ Exchange:_____

DATE	BUY @ PRICE	BUY AMOUNT	WEIGHT	SELL @ PRICE	SELL AMOUNT	PROFIT/LOSS

METAL/TYPE:_____ Exchange:_____

DATE	BUY @ PRICE	BUY AMOUNT	WEIGHT	SELL @ PRICE	SELL AMOUNT	PROFIT/LOSS

METAL/TYPE:_____ Exchange:_____

DATE	BUY @ PRICE	BUY AMOUNT	WEIGHT	SELL @ PRICE	SELL AMOUNT	PROFIT/LOSS

METAL/TYPE:_____ Exchange:_____

DATE	BUY @ PRICE	BUY AMOUNT	WEIGHT	SELL @ PRICE	SELL AMOUNT	PROFIT/LOSS

METAL/TYPE:_____ Exchange:_____

DATE	BUY @ PRICE	BUY AMOUNT	WEIGHT	SELL @ PRICE	SELL AMOUNT	PROFIT/LOSS

METAL/TYPE:_____ Exchange:_____

DATE	BUY @ PRICE	BUY AMOUNT	WEIGHT	SELL @ PRICE	SELL AMOUNT	PROFIT/LOSS